Ken Freeman h
of evangelism I
and favored to communicate Jesus' gospel to any and
all ages. His life is a tribute to faithfulness, integrity, and
passion for God's church. You are one choice away
from reading a life-changing book!

—Pastor Shannon O'Dell
Pastor, Brand New Church, Bergman Arkansas
Author, *Transforming Churches in Rural America*

Evangelist and author Ken Freeman speaks to
hundreds of thousands of people each year. It has been
an honor of mine to get to know Ken through the
multiple events we have done together each year since
2000. Now, in his new book *Choices 101*, Ken reveals
how the choices of those around him dramatically
affected his life. God has truly taken the horrific mess of
Ken's childhood and turned it into a message of hope
and redemption. Through his real-life experiences we
can learn that even though other people's choices may
bring us challenges, ultimately our own choices will
determine our destiny. We must always remember that
we are all "one choice away from a different life."

—Rev. Dean Forrest
Big God Conferences
2012 President of the Conference of
Southern Baptist Evangelists

Choices 101 is something I have heard my father speak about for years. As a son, youth minister, associate pastor, and now senior pastor, I have seen God powerfully communicate the truths in this book, through Ken Freeman, to impact countless lives for Christ. Each day, we make hundreds of choices, and the choices we make impact every aspect of our lives. In *Choices 101*, Ken Freeman will challenge you, in whatever stage of life you are in, to make choices that will have profound influence for the Kingdom of God. As he always says, "You are one choice away from a different life." That statement is absolutely true, and one of the greatest choices you could make would be to purchase the book, read it, and then share it with as many people as possible. You and those who read *Choices 101* will forever be changed!

—Rev. Jeremy Freeman
Senior Pastor, First Baptist Church
Newcastle, OK

Ken Freeman

CHOICES 101

You're One Choice Away from a Different Life

TOUCH
PUBLISHING

Choices 101
Copyright © 2013 2017 Ken Freeman

ISBN: 978-1-942508-36-6

Published by Touch Publishing
P.O. Box 180303
Arlington, Texas 76096 U.S.A.
www.TouchPublishingServices.com
Edited by Kimberly Soesbee

Scripture quotations are taken from the Holy Bible, New Living Translation, copyright ©1996. Used by permission of Tyndale House Publishers, Inc., Wheaton, Illinois 60189.

1. Religion / Christian Life / Personal Growth
2. Religion / Christian Life / Spiritual Growth
17.08.01

Library of Congress Control Number: 2017950064

DEDICATION

This book is dedicated to my father-in-law,
Ted Tedder, a Hebrews 11 hero of faith. He chose
to love God, his wife, daughters, grandchildren,
and great-grandchildren. He chose to serve his country.
Ted died in July of 2011. My wife was there to watch as
he took his last breath. Ted Tedder was an incredible
man of God! His funeral was awesome!

I dedicate this book to a man that always chose
to do what was right. We need more Ted Tedders
in our world.

ACKNOWLEDGEMENTS

I'm grateful to My Father, Savior, Lord, and Best Friend who chose to love and adopt me into His family, thank you, Jesus! Ephesians 1:3-8.

This special thank you is for my in-laws. I'm thankful to my wife's parents, Ted and Billie Tedder. They gave me their wonderful daughter to be my wife, and they were great examples of Jesus!

I'm thankful to my Jesus-Parents: Malcolm and Johnnie Grainger, for choosing to take me into their home my senior year in high school—that choice changed my life.

I'm thankful to my wife for choosing to be my wife and for supporting me for over thirty years as I've traveled on the road sharing the good news of Jesus Christ. She's an incredible wife, mom, and grandma (Gaga). She is a gift of God. Philippians 1:8.

I'm thankful to Jeff, the football player who chose to invite me to church and share Jesus with me. His choice to get me to church saved my life! Luke 5:17-25.

I'm thankful for my two sons and grandkids who have loaned me out to others so I can share Jesus!

I'm thankful for Castle Hills First Baptist Church for giving me my Spiritual Roots of Faith.

Thank you to the great ministers of the Gospel who pour into my life: Jack Taylor, Manley Beasley, Ron

Dunn, Peter Lord, Bertha Smith, Adrian Rogers, Ronnie Floyd, Jerry Sutton, and my pastor, Robert Emmit.

I'm thankful for Freddie Gage, the evangelist I was saved under. I'm thankful for all the churches that have chosen to let me minster in their churches! I'm thankful to Jay Hall and Dave King for believing in me and my ministry and birthing my Wild Week Camps.

I'm thankful for Harold Hanusch and Kacy Benson for the honor to serve and minister with them. These guys are a couple of my best friends.

Thank you to Dean Forest and Big God Ministries.

I appreciate Dean, Gayna, and Geoffrey, and I am thankful for their belief in my ministry. I'm, very thankful to Karla Bosarge for her patience and gift to help me write this book. You took the words right out of my mouth. Great job.

All of these people and more have made choices to help me in my life and ministry!

The choices we make every day will always affect people around us in a good way or a bad way. Take time to thank people in your life who choose to believe in you. The choices we make today determine how we will live tomorrow!

I choose to keep following Jesus!

TABLE OF CONTENTS

Introduction

Choices 101—sounds like a class. Sounds like a school project. Well, let me tell you this, "Choices" *is* a class. The rest of your life you're going to be in class, and I want to talk to you about the types of choices you make that affect four main aspects of your life—family, friends, future, and faith. Remember, you're one choice away from a different life.

Choices 101: it's a class we wake up to every day. Do you know the most powerful thing you do in your life each day? It's not making money. It's not being a great athlete, the smartest kid in your school, the best parent, or a great businessperson. The most powerful thing you were created to do was not be successful, not be popular, and not be prominent or powerful. Instead, the most powerful thing you do in your life is make choices. In fact, you're making a choice right now in reading this book.

I want to encourage you to understand that you were created more uniquely than any other living creature, because you have the power to choose. In fact, when you woke up this morning, you began your day

1

making all types of choices. You chose your attitude; the very first thing you chose when you woke up was whether you would be negative or positive today. Would you obey your parents today? Would you do your best in class? Would you get along with your family today? Would you serve today? Would you choose to make today a good day? If you woke up today and chose to have a negative attitude, then you chose for your day to go badly. However, if you woke up and chose to make today a good day, then you decided from the very beginning that you were not going to sweat the small stuff.

Not only did you choose your attitude, you made a dozen other small choices before you even made it out of the house. You chose to brush your teeth (thankfully). You chose what type of toothbrush to use. You chose your toothpaste. You chose to use deodorant (hopefully). You chose the type of deodorant you would use. You chose to brush your hair (maybe).

Do you understand that before you even get out of bed, you choose your attitude? Choosing your attitude is a powerful choice. You choose (or maybe you don't) to clean yourself up before you go out into a dirty world. You choose what you're going to wear. You choose what you're going to eat. You choose friendships and relationships. You choose what direction you're going to go, how you're going to talk, how you're going to live. You choose the music you listen to, the movies and TV shows you watch. You choose whom you text, what you say on Facebook and Twitter, the videos you watch on YouTube, and which websites you visit on the Internet.

Every day you make choices. Four things are always affected by the choices you make. Family, friendships, future, faith. In this book, I am going to share with you some of my own story and how my personal choices affected my friends, family, future, and faith. I am going to provide you with personal examples of people in my life, as well as people who are well-known in today's world who have made choices that have also affected their families, their friends, their future, and their faith.

The greatest understanding I want you to take away from reading this book is that you were created with the power to choose every day. By your reading this book, I want you to come away knowing the choices you make also affect your friends, family, future, and faith. Choices 101 is a class we take every day of our lives, whether you believe it or not. I want to encourage you today to choose to make powerful choices.

This is an interactive book, and throughout it you will find a series of questions pertaining to your life and what you have read in the book so far.

Below each question or statement, you will see lines for you to fill in your response. Think of this book as a study guide. As you read, I encourage you to have a pen with you, so that you may think more deeply about your life and the choices that affect you and others. This book is different from other devotional-type books in that you will have multiple opportunities within chapters to respond, instead of just at the end of the chapter. I hope you take a lot away from this book, and that you reflect not only on the message of the book, but on your own choices as well.

The Power of One Choice

"You're one choice away from a different life."

This quote brings to mind a story I recently saw on national news. A fourteen-year-old girl had three friends over for a sleepover. Everything was going great, but then the girls started experimenting with alcohol. They got a bottle of vodka and began drinking it with coke. The next morning, the three friends who had stayed over tried to wake the girl up, but she wouldn't wake up. At fourteen years old, she died of alcohol poisoning. I doubt she thought when she had her friends over that night that her choice to drink alcohol would lead her to death by the night's end.

Look at these celebrities as examples: Tiger Woods. Charlie Sheen. Britney Spears. Michael Jackson. Arnold Schwarzenegger. These are just a few of the "successful" people in the world whose choices have affected their lives in huge ways. They each made choices that changed their lives. Just like these celebrities, one choice can change the course of not

5

only your life, but the lives of those around you. I have learned this first-hand as I watched simple choices change the lives of family members and friends. Some people made choices that positively impacted their lives. However, most of the people I knew growing up made choices that not only negatively affected them, but their families as well.

I grew up in an unstable home. I never knew what type of day I would have because I didn't know what my mom's choices would be. You see every choice you make affects your family. Would my mom choose to be drunk in the morning or when I got home from school? Usually, the answer was yes.

My mom never sobered up enough to choose to put her children first. Instead, even from childhood, I knew no stable life. Would I come home to a passed-out mom or would I come home to a mom who beat me with a stick? Either of these situations could be the case. Would I have dinner tonight? Maybe.

Because of my mom's choice to drink alcohol, her family was affected in a major way. My younger sister and I went hungry, transferred schools often, and didn't ever know where a permanent home was. We never stayed in one place long enough to make lifetime friends. People talk about having the same best friend since kindergarten; neither my sister nor I had this opportunity. We weren't given the chance to build relationships with our peers, because as soon as someone started to accept us, we moved again. Mom's choices led to broken relationships between herself and uncountable men, her children and their classmates, but most importantly, Mom's choices led to broken, seemingly irreparable relationships between her children and herself. Because of my mom's one choice—the choice to drink—my sister and I suffered in unimaginable ways.

Maybe you come from background like mine. Maybe you didn't have the best parent. Then again, maybe you did. Maybe you came from one of those homes I only saw on TV, where there was a happily married mom and dad. Either way, your parents' choices affected you either positively or negatively.

1. What type of parent(s) do/did you have? How do/did your parent(s') choices affect you?

_____

_____

_____

_____

Tiger Woods, like my mom so many others, also made a choice that affected his family negatively. From what the world saw, Tiger had everything. He had a successful golf career at which he earned millions of dollars in cash and endorsements. He had fame—everyone knew his name. Everyone wanted to be the next Tiger Woods—rich, famous, and seemingly happy. Tiger had a beautiful wife and two loving children. He had everything a man could want and all the money to "buy" happiness, if such a thing was possible. If he wanted to go to the most expensive restaurant, money was no object. He could buy any toy he wanted. The biggest house. The biggest boat. If money could buy happiness and success, Tiger Woods would be one of the happiest, most successful men on the planet.

But sometimes things aren't what they seem. Tiger Woods, who seemed to be making all the right choices, achieved more in his life than most people ever dream of accomplishing. Tiger had more money than he knew what to do with. Not only that, but he had the fame associated with being the greatest golfer to ever play the game. Every golf and sporting company wanted to say that Tiger Woods represented their product. People wanted to be as "successful" as Tiger, the man who had it all. But even someone as seemingly invincible as Tiger Woods can change his or her world with just one choice.

With one choice Tiger Woods affected his family in a huge way. Tiger chose to be unfaithful to his marriage vows, and he lost everything. By choosing to bed dozens of women, Tiger destroyed his marriage and his relationship with his wife and family. Tiger's choice, like my mom's choice, affected his family. His family would never be the secure, two-parent, mom and dad unit it had been prior to Tiger's choice to break his marriage vows. Tiger chose to corrupt his marriage with lies and deception. Tiger could have lived his life rich, happy, and famous if he had chosen to remain faithful to his wife. One choice changed everything. Tiger rocked his world with one bad choice.

Every choice you make has either a positive or a negative impact on those you care about the most. You may not have children, but you have a family. You have someone who cares about you. Maybe it's your parents, maybe not. Maybe a sister or a brother. All of these people are affected by your choices.

2. List the people in your family who are affected by your choices.

_____

_____

_____

_____

Another celebrity who suffered a public collapse is famous for his public meltdowns and poor choices. Charlie Sheen, one of the highest paid actors on television, who earned 1.8 million dollars per episode on CBS's *Two and a Half Men* had a very public meltdown in early 2011. He went on television shows, the Internet, and radio talk shows, displaying an array of erratic behavior—he ranted about his job, his life, and anything else that bothered him. The world watched as this apparently crazy man broke down. People watched Charlie Sheen melt down as a form of entertainment. Everyone wanted to know what Charlie would do next.

Much like Tiger Woods and my mom, Charlie Sheen made choices that negatively affected his family. For over twenty years, Charlie Sheen's name has been attached to drug scandals. Charlie Sheen's drug use set him on a cycle, or a path, to destruction. Charlie Sheen has been married three times and has five different children. His first daughter was born to his former high school girlfriend. After that relationship ended, Charlie became engaged to another woman whom he accidentally shot in the arm.

In the middle of the 90s, Charlie married yet another woman who divorced him after his name was released as a high profile client for an escort agency. In the early 2000s, Charlie married Denise Richards and they had two children, but she too filed for divorce, citing Charlie's excessive alcohol and drug use as well as violent threats.

Most recently, Charlie Sheen was married to

Brooke Mueller, with whom he had twins. Charlie Sheen filed for divorce yet again in November 2010, but the divorce didn't finalize until May 2, 2011. In the meantime, Charlie lived with two girlfriends, who he referred to as "goddesses." Charlie's life spun out of control in a downhill spiral. At one point, Charlie's behavior became so unpredictable that police removed his youngest two children from his home, and his twin sons' mother had a straining order placed against him.

Charlie Sheen's choice to take drugs led to deep divisions in his family life. His children watched as their father turned to drugs and sexual relationships to cope. Much like Tiger Woods, Charlie has destroyed his family relationships.

If Charlie Sheen had made the right choices, his life would not be in a repeat pattern of negativity. Maybe one day he can build better relationships with his five children, but from what the world can see, he chooses to repeat the same mistakes that have gotten him nothing but trouble over the years. Charlie's children have to live with the stigma associated with their father's name. They watch as their dad abuses drugs, has public meltdowns, and has many broken relationships with women.

3. Do you think about your family when you make choices, or are you like Tiger, Charlie, or my mom?

11

What choices do you make that affect your family?

_____

_____

_____

_____

How will your actions affect those you should care about the most? Your actions should reflect that you care about your family, but if they don't, you need to reevaluate the choices you make. You can choose to make positive choices, or you can choose to make negative choices that adversely affect your family. You can be like the girl I mentioned at the beginning of the chapter, who died of alcohol poisoning at fourteen, or you can make the choice not to put yourself in dangerous situations. What will you choose?

4. Take a moment and think about the choices you make that affect others. List at least four positive choices you can make to impact your family.

_____

_____

_____

_____

Choosing Teams

"Show me your friends, and I'll show you your future."

Thursday. Gym class is now in session. Your class plays softball on Thursdays. Your coach chooses you and another student to pick teams. You begin calling out names one at a time. You want the best players on your team, so you strategically call out names, ensuring that your team is the best.

But have you ever been on the flip side of that? The last one chosen? You know softball Thursday is here, and softball may not be your sport. Two kids begin picking teams, a time you dread. You watch as students are chosen one by one, but you don't hear your name. Finally, the pool of students narrows down to two—you and the kid with the broken leg. You think, "Oh good, I will finally be chosen." Then Team Captain 1 chooses the kid with the broken leg.

You are not chosen. It's not the first time, and it may not be the last, but it hurts. It may be funny to imagine yourself not being chosen for softball over the kid with the broken leg, but maybe you've been in a similar situation where you were the last one chosen. And I know the feeling, because I've been there too— the last person left—the kid not chosen. For me, those were some of the toughest moments of my childhood.

1. *Have you ever been the kid not chosen? Or were you always the chooser? Describe a time in your life when you were either choosing or you were chosen.*

_____

_____

_____

_____

_____

As an alcoholic, my mom never chose me. When I was little, Mom might sometimes drop off a bag of fast food burgers or a bucket of fried chicken for my sister and me on Friday, which sounds great, right? But we were kids, and we wouldn't see her again until late Sunday night. Mom spent my childhood drunk—she went to bed drunk, woke up drunk, and even went to work drunk. My mom chose alcohol and drugs over her children. Rather than choosing my sister and I for her team, she chose substance abuse. It isn't the same thing as not being chosen for a softball team, but I can tell you

I do know what it's like to not be chosen. Growing up, I went to twenty-four different schools, including five different high schools my senior year. Because of this, I never really got a chance to get to know people very well. The other kids already had their close-knit group of friends that made it difficult for me to infiltrate their social groups. So when we played games, it didn't matter what game we played, I was the last kid chosen—or as I like to put it, the kid not chosen.

The first few kids chosen always got called by their names.

"Tom."

"James."

"Kenny."

This went on for a few rounds of choices, and then one of the captains would call a girl's name. *But she's a girl!* I would think to myself, as the feeling inside my chest grew tighter, and the disappointment would grow. Though I had been in this situation before, I still remained hopeful that my name would get called.

After all the good players had been called, the team captains stopped using names, and then the pointing began.

"I got you, over there in the red shirt."

Or "I got the guy with the glasses."

When the pool of kids to choose from narrowed down to three or four, and the others got pointed and added to teams, it came down to two—me and the tree.

Hope turned to disappointment, or a feeling of worthlessness.

What's even worse, no one even pointed at me to add me to his or her team. I would stand there alone, hoping to be chosen, with longing in my heart. Unfortunately, this would not be the case.

You know what happened? The two teams would turn and walk away, leaving me behind. Not that I wasn't used to being walked away from. It still hurt. No matter how many times the same situation played out over and over, the pain burned the same way each time.

As far as this softball game was concerned, I could either follow the team that didn't call the last pick, or I could leave. Not only was I the kid with no name, I was the kid no one wanted to choose.

When you're the last one standing, you don't even get pointed at. You don't get chosen. Someone's choice affected you.

*2. Think back on the same example you gave for #1.
How does it feel to be chosen? How does it feel to be the kid not chosen?*

_____

_____

_____

_____

For all of my life, people walked away from me, and I don't just mean on the ball field or court. My dad walked out of my life when I was four. I lived with an alcoholic mom who "walked out" on me every time she took another drink. The nine stepfathers that came and went, along with dozens of other men walking out of my mom's life made me know what being "not chosen" was. None of my "dads" chose me.

I lived in bars, on the streets, in cars, in taverns. Always the new kid at school, I never got chosen for anything. Never got chosen for the spelling bee. Never got a ribbon. I certainly didn't win an attendance award. Yet, I *wanted* to be a winner. I *wanted* to be chosen. You know what? I just wanted somebody to pick me to be on his or her team.

Have you been there? Not chosen? Maybe for a simple game or maybe for something far more significant. What does not being chosen do to you as a person? I can tell you. You don't feel like you fit in. You don't feel talented. You may not have much money. Your parents may not have the best life. I've been there, too. Maybe you come from my background or a background just as miserable.

Maybe you come from a broken home. Statistics show that forty percent of children come from a divorced home. Also, twenty-four million kids in America live in a home in which the biological father is absent. This translates to one in every three kids you know is living without their real dad in their home. Thirty-eight million kids in America have no idea where their real father is. I would guess that about half of the people I speak to come from broken homes. Nineteen million kids have never seen their real dad.

3. Reflect on who you live with. Who are your "parents"? Is your home a happy place? Why or why not?

_____

_____

_____

     Maybe you come from a background like mine and you know how it feels not to be chosen. But maybe you come from an incredible background. Maybe you're the kid who always gets to choose. You know what you ought to do? For once in your life, choose someone else to choose. Be the person who gives that kid who never gets chosen a chance. Choose to have a positive impact on someone's life.

4. List people who come to mind. How can you positively impact those people?

_____

_____

_____

Every day we're choosing teams. Who are we going to play for? Who are we going to play with? How are we going to play? In all of this, we have to make positive choices. Our choices are not just affected by the team we choose to be on. That is, if we choose the wrong friends, we might lead ourselves down the path to destruction. We may ruin our lives just as my mom ruined hers by choosing to drink and choosing to be on the wrong team.

"Show me your friends, and I'll show you your future."

As I grew up and watched the men come and go from my mom's life, I also watched friends lead her down the road to destruction. At fifteen, my mom chose to take her first drink of alcohol. What she didn't realize was that a choice she made at fifteen would kill her at fifty-two. She didn't know that by choosing to be on the team that abused substances, she would destroy her life as well as the lives of her children. Alcohol controlled her actions.

As a kid, when I went to bed at night, I never knew what to expect. My mom would drag my sister and I out of bed at night to beat us on the back of the legs with a broomstick. The broomstick is not your typical "switch" or paddle. It is thick, hard, rounded, and it is meant to cause great pain and leave bruises.

Typically, my mom would beat me first, choosing to take her anger out on me. Then, she would snatch my little sister, Donna, from her bed and throw her forcefully across the room, into a wall. After that, she would choose to beat Donna too. After Mom hit and beat on Donna for a while, I would eventually place my body in between the two, blocking my sister with my arms so Mom would stop hitting her. Reaching around me, Mom would get in a few more slaps before she would give up and eventually leave the room.

Donna and I lived in fear each time Mom left. We'd sleep by the front door of our house, fully dressed. We did this so we could listen for Mom's car to pull up at two or three a.m. When we heard her, we knew we could slip out the back door to avoid her drunken rage. My sister and I would then finish out the night in backyards, garages, streets, alleys, parks, or open cars. We were looking for a way to escape.

5. Have you ever looked for an escape? What did you do?

_____

_____

_____

_____

By the time I was ten, we lived in Hazelwood, Missouri; basically St. Louis. One night, I woke up with a butcher knife to my throat. I thought I was dreaming for sure. I could hear Donna crying, and I could feel the metal against my neck. I thought, *Man, this is more than a dream.* I could smell the whiskey on my mom's breath as she held the knife to my throat. My blood ran cold, and I thought that night would be my last. My mom threatened to kill us. This wasn't the only time she made such a threat. I begged my mom not to kill me.

I begged her not to kill Donna. I don't know if I begged hard enough or what, but my mom eventually dropped the knife and passed out in my bed. She had chosen once again to let the alcohol control her. My sister and I got to live one more day.

Sometimes, Mom would get so mad at us that she would put us in the backseat of her car and drive to wherever she felt like driving. She would stop on the side of the road, in a parking lot, or wherever she felt like stopping. She'd pull us out of the car and say, "Now you stay there until I come back and get you." It could be thirty minutes, three hours, six hours, sometimes all night. Donna and I never knew when or even if Mom would choose to come back for her children. We didn't know if we would ever be going home again.

Sure, Mom would have wild parties, and her "friends" would come hang out with her—they loved coming over for nights of drunkenness. They were looking for a good time. But where were they when Mom was passed-out drunk? Where were they when she was dying?

The type of people my mother considered "friends" did not stick with her when times were rough. They were fair weather friends—only there when something exciting and fun was going on. If alcohol or drugs was involved, these "friends" were there. But when my mom died, her "friends" were nowhere to be found. As my mom's death neared, I watched her lay in a bed for weeks, her body weakening.

For some people, death is quick. For others, death comes slowly and painfully. For my mom, dying was very painful. My mom was diagnosed with cirrhosis of the liver. Cirrhosis of the liver is caused by years of being an alcoholic. The liver performs over four hundred functions for the body's overall health, and it can process only so much abuse before it shuts down.

Since my mom was an alcoholic from the age of fifteen, her liver had fought through a lifetime of abuse. Eventually, my mom's liver began shutting down on her. While my mom continued abusing her body, her liver could no longer take it. When the liver shuts down, then the rest of the body shuts down with it.

As my mom went through the dying process, I watched her eyes bleed red and her skin turn yellow. I watched her body deteriorate. Where were her friends or all the men my mom chose for her team? They did not come. Instead, my mom lay in bed for six weeks in pain, with her body shutting down. She didn't have a lot of visitors. She chose the wrong team. You know what happened to my mom? At the end of those painful six weeks, she died.

6. Do you know someone who has suffered consequences for their choices? Death? Punishment? Something else? Write about the consequences of that person's actions.

_____

_____

_____

_____

I tried for fourteen years to convince my mom to make better choices. But I couldn't choose for her. If I had been able to choose for my mom, then she would have changed her life and never have taken another drink. Instead, my mom chose to continue drinking alcohol. She chose to move on from husband to husband to boyfriend. She chose what team she belonged to. She drowned in alcohol.

7. *Are you choosing the right team? Or are you choosing friends that lead you to destroy yourself? Who are your friends? Are they true friends? Explain how you are either choosing the right team or the wrong team.*

_____

_____

_____

_____

_____

8. *Explain how you can eliminate some of the negative choices in your life. How will your life be made better by these choices?*

_____

_____

_____

_____

_____

The Garden of Choices

"Everyone has a Garden of Eden."

Make powerful choices! You are presented with opportunities every single day to either live a good life or to make choices that lead you down a negative path. Don't be the dad who walks out on his family. Don't be the friend who leads others into lives of addiction.

Life is a garden of choices. Each day, you have the opportunity to make either good or bad decisions. Make sure that your choices positively affect those around you. Make your garden a nourishing and strong place.

Have you ever been affected negatively by someone's choices? I know I have. I mentioned my mom's garden of choices earlier. She chose alcohol. She left us home alone often, but sometimes she did get us a babysitter. In a perfect world, your babysitter is an Aunt Bea, grandmotherly type, who loves kids. Unfortunately, this was not my reality, and our babysitter wasn't nurturing at all.

One night, my sister and I were left with one of

my mom's ex-boyfriends while she chose to live another drunken weekend. You see, at our house, people came to party and pass out. I remember lying down to go to sleep when my mom came in and said, "Hey, I'll see you in three days." Then she left. Twenty minutes after Mom's car pulled out of the driveway, I heard my baby sister screaming. I looked over the bunk bed, expecting to see her thrashing from a nightmare or a dream. She had nightmares often, but this was not the case that night. Instead, I saw a man, our babysitter for the weekend, in the bed with Donna.

My mom chose to leave her kids with an ex-boyfriend while she went and partied. This ex-boyfriend chose to rape my five-year-old sister. I didn't know what rape was or what the man was doing to Donna, but I knew that whatever it was—it was wrong. I didn't know what to do, so I yelled at the dude to stop. I didn't know what was going on, but with my sister screaming like that, I knew it had to be bad. I yelled at the man, "Hey! Stop! Leave her alone!" The man grabbed me by the arm and dragged me down from my bunk. The anger I felt at him for hurting Donna suddenly turned to fear. As a seven-year-old, I didn't know how to fight this adult who was supposed to be responsible for me. I didn't know how to fight this "babysitter" who was supposed to take care of us. Instead, that night, my mom's ex raped Donna and molested me.

26

When my mom came home three days later, I wanted so badly to tell her what happened. She walked in the front door, and I started to tell her what I thought happened, but I couldn't think of what to say. The cretin who'd hurt us was standing right there, with a bottle of alcohol in his hand, so I couldn't speak. I didn't know what he would do if I said it in front of him. He might deny it or he might do it again. As a seven-year old, I felt intense fear when I looked at him. Mom made it easy for me not to speak. She made it easy for me to keep it in, because she was so drunk, she went back in the bedroom and passed out. The man got in his car and left.

Days later, I still waited for my mom to wake up so I could tell her. Something was wrong with Donna. When Mom finally woke up, she reached immediately for a bottle. I told her, "Before you get drunk, I gotta tell you something." My sister was still crying, and so was I. We couldn't explain what had happened to us. We were just kids, so I looked at my mom and told her the best I could what happened. Her facial expression turned to panic, and she threw on a robe and snatched us up. She made us get in the car, and she drove us to the hospital. The doctors examined my sister and me. It had been worse for Donna than it had been for me. Donna had to stay in the hospital, but I was released.

From the hospital, my mom took me to the police station. The cops took me back into the room with the glass where they line up criminals. The cops held me, a seven year old, up to the window to pick out of a lineup the man who had done these things.

I looked for a moment at the men standing there, then pointed, "There, that's him. That's the guy who did those things." The man went to jail for what he did to us. His actions had consequences. He chose to be a sex offender, and he had to pay a price for it. Not only was his life changed because he was now labeled a sexual predator or a pedophile, but Donna's and my lives were changed as well. This man's choice had combined with my mom's choice to affect my sister and me in harmful ways. Donna and I both struggled with how to make positive choices for a long time afterward. I would eventually make a positive choice to change my future, but my sister would not.

1. Do you have hurts from your childhood that still affect you? What positive choices are you making each day to make your life successful?

_____

_____

_____

_____

2. Is there a bad choice you've made that has affected everything in your life? What was it? If not, write about a time that you could have made a bad choice, but chose to do what was right.

_____

_____

_____

_____

You are one choice away from a different life. I said that my sister was not as fortunate as I was in her garden of choices. I found her in 1998, and it shocked me to see that she had turned into the one she hated the most—our mom. So much of her life paralleled to that of Mom's. Shocked, I could see how I could have gone down the same path, but I didn't. Whereas positive choices led me to become who I am today, my sister made the choice to turn to substance abuse just like Mom.

The first time I saw my sister after many years, she was either drunk or stoned or both, and she was very bitter. She couldn't possibly weigh seventy pounds, and I guessed with a generous estimate that she had maybe twelve teeth in her mouth. Before I met up with Donna, she had already been diagnosed with Hepatitis C and cirrhosis of the liver. She had also had many relationships with men, just like Mom. I kept in touch with her, keeping up with her, helping her financially. Donna needed money to pay her bills, so I gave her that. Donna also needed extensive dental work, so I helped her financially with that as well. It was easy to help my sister financially, but Donna needed more help than I could give. Nonetheless, I wanted to be there for her as much as I could. Money doesn't fix every problem. Sure, with financial assistance, Donna could pay bills and get a new smile, but Donna's issues ran deeper than money. I couldn't just walk out on my sister. Even though she made bad choices, her tie to me remained because she was still my sister. You can't choose your family, and you can't choose the paths for their lives, but you can be there for them.

3. Is there someone in your family, like my mom or sister whose choices are leading them in the wrong direction? What can you do for them?

_____

_____

_____

_____

    Donna loved to help others. Even though she herself needed help, more help than any human can give, she gave generously to people she considered her "friends." Anytime one of these "friends" needed a favor, Donna gave them her time, attention, and anything she had. She always opened her home and her heart to these people. Unfortunately, the "friends" she chose to help, the ones she cared so deeply about, were the same ones who dragged her down into a life of despair. These "friends" encouraged her lifestyle of drug addiction and alcoholism. They participated in the same hurtful habits that Donna did, and they agreed with her negative lifestyle choices because they were making the same choices Donna made.

4. Who are your friends? List people you consider to be your closest friends.

_____

_____

_____

One night, I received a terrifying phone call from Donna. As she sat in her alcohol-ridden apartment in the St. Louis projects, she had determined that the only way out the hell she lived in was to kill herself and her son. I begged Donna to wait at least twenty-four hours before making that choice. I was so worried for them. Death seemed to be an easier option than life for her. Donna was looking for a way to escape. Ultimately, she did not take her life that night, yet she continued to suffer from the diseases she brought upon herself. She suffered emotionally. Donna let my mom's choices affect her lifestyle in a huge and negative way. Looking at Donna was like looking at a broken record—watching my mom's mistakes repeated over and over again.

A few years later, my sister died after drinking vodka and taking too much pain medication. This overdose may have been intentional—I can't be sure, but I assume that it was. The pain of her diseases along with her depression may have been too much for my baby sister. It hurts to see someone you love spiral down the familiar path of destruction, and I watched helplessly as Donna followed my mom's choices straight into the grave.

I could have ended up like my sister. My mom's choice to be a poor mother affected my sister in a completely different way than it did me. Where were my sister's friends when she died? The ones who encouraged her negative lifestyle were nowhere in sight when my baby sister left this earth. Show me your friends, and I'll show you your future.

5. How do your friends' choices affect you? Do your friends make good choices? Are they encouragers, or are they leading you down a destructive path?

Don't you choose who you talk to? You have a garden of choices in front of you each day at school, at work, in your neighborhood, and now even online or through text messaging. What about Facebook? Are the people you "friend" on Facebook really your friends? If you click "Accept" to someone's friend request, does that really make you that person's friend? Would you tell that person everything about you?

6. What makes a true friend?

Choosing Facebook friends may seem like such an insignificant choice compared to the big picture. In the garden of choices, Charlie Sheen and Tiger Woods had a lot of options as well. Earlier I discussed how Tiger could have chosen to stay true to his marriage vows and preserve his family. If Tiger had not slept with so many women, then maybe his future would be different. Now for the rest of his life, he will be paying millions of dollars to his ex-wife because of his choice. His kids live in the bounds of a custody agreement because their dad cheated on their mom. Broken homes are becoming the norm in today's world, and I hope you don't let other people's choices affect how you will live your life.

In the Garden of Choices, you can choose to sleep with many different people at a young age. TV shows like *The Secret Life of the American Teenager*, *Glee*, and *Pretty Little Liars* tell you this is normal, that as long as you feel good for a moment, then you are doing the right thing.

7. Think about the TV shows you watch, what you do on the internet, and the music you listen to. What message are these things sending you? Is it positive? List a show, song, or website you frequent and describe the message it sends?

_____

_____

_____

_____

From pop culture you may get the picture that you can do what you want, with whom you want, and there are no consequences. These television shows along with music and movies don't present the truth and consequences that a single choice can have. Teenage pregnancy is not anything to be glamorized. STDs are a big deal, yet television tells you that as long as you feel good for a moment, you're doing the right thing. But you know you're not. You need to realize that one seemingly small bad choice can lead to a lifetime of negativity. Be careful with your choices. Be aware of what you're doing each time you make a decision.

8. Are the choices you make today having a positive impact on your family, friends, and future? Explain why or why not.

My choices affect my family positively/negatively because:

_____

_____

_____

My friends' choices affect me positively/negatively because:

_____

_____

_____

My future is affected positively/negatively in these ways:

_____

_____

_____

In my own garden of choices, there were several times when I made the wrong choice. I mentioned earlier that we are all just one choice away from a different life. As a nine-year-old, I took an entire bottle of aspirin, hoping for an escape from my pain. I don't know if I wanted to die, but I do know I made a conscious choice that could have changed everything. I just wanted to stop the hurt.

I wanted the pills to take me away from the negativity of my life, away from a mom who beat me, away from memories of a dad who didn't want me. Like Donna, who would later overdose, I almost took myself out of this life as a nine-year-old. It could have resulted in my never having really lived. I didn't see life as being worth the living. I can imagine how Donna felt as an adult living in public housing without any financial stability.

9. Is there a time in your past in which you didn't see that life was worth living? What happened?
   If not, what can you do to positively impact someone else by letting them know their life is worth living and that you value them? Who is placed on your heart?

_____

_____

_____

At another time in my garden of choices, I had the opportunity to make the wrong choice, but instead, I made the right choice. My mom was passed out on the kitchen floor after coming in from a long night of drinking. I remember being emotionally and physically exhausted as I stood over her body, staring down at her on the cold kitchen floor. I was tired of her abuse; tired of her alcohol addiction. I wanted her to feel some of the pain she inflicted on Donna and me. All the hate and anger from years of abuse and neglect welled up inside of me. Rage, like I had never felt before, consumed me.

I realized as I looked at her that I wanted her dead. I grabbed a butcher knife from the counter. As its handle melded together with the warm flesh of my hand, I contemplated murder.

She deserved it.

Death should be her punishment for all she put me through. With the knife in my hand, I ran the silver blade of the knife up and down my mother's body. Hands shaking, sobbing, I longed to kill her. I could pay her back for everything she had ever done to me. I could get revenge. I had a choice to make.

I did not become a murderer that night. I don't know why I didn't do it. I dropped the knife on the kitchen floor without even cutting her. Then I turned and ran out through the front door, screaming.

You're one choice away from a better life or a bitter life.

10. Like me, have you ever been so angry that you almost did something regretful? Write about that time.

My sister and I had completely different futures, because we are all just one choice away from a different life. Donna chose the way of destruction. She followed in Mom's footsteps and it led her down the exact path that Mom had followed, and eventually she suffered from the same disease that killed Mom. Unlike Mom and Donna, I chose to change my future when I was in high school. I chose to go to church with my friend Jeff, and I've never been the same. That one choice set a series of events into motion that led me down a completely different path. I could have lived a bitter life. I could have been the kid who grew up to be the next junkie or another child abuser, but here I am writing to you today about one positive choice that changed me forever.

11. Do you see your life as a Garden of Choices? What are some choices you make that affect your future?

Changing Directions

There came a time in my life when I had to take control of my future. I changed directions, so not only did my future change, but my faith changed drastically as well. By the time I got to high school, I started making some poor choices of my own. I started living like my mom. I started doing my drug of choice—alcohol. I looked for anything I could to erase my memory of the negativity in my life. Just like as a nine-year-old I tried to escape life by swallowing a bottle of aspirin, I looked for any way or anything to dull the pain of living. I wanted to find peace. I decided at one point that I needed a change, so I moved with one of my stepdads to Corpus Christi, Texas. I moved there with him and my two step-brothers. I wanted to get away from a mom I hated. I thought my life would get better once I was away from her. Eventually, this stepdad married a different woman. Then, she started beating up on me. I said, "I ain't doing this again." I didn't put up with it. I made the choice to leave yet another abusive situation. I packed everything I owned into a suitcase and left. Homeless, I wandered all over Corpus Christi. I stayed wherever families would let me stay. One family might let me stay two to three days. Another a week. I had no home. My future was bleak as I relied on the charity of others to survive. I didn't know how long I could rely on the generosity of others, but it was the only future I could see.

1. Have you ever needed an escape or a change? What did you do?

_____

_____

_____

I wandered around Corpus Christi for a while without direction. Then, I met Jeff. I hated Jeff. Jeff was a football player who loved God. I mean, he would tackle you for Jesus. The dude was insane. I'd met Christians before. Most of them were lifeless, but Jeff was very much alive. Jeff had a little bit in common with me. He had a gutless dad who walked out of his life, too. So Jeff knew what it was like to grow up without a father. Unlike me, Jeff had a godly mom who cared about him and who wanted him to succeed in life. She didn't collapse or become an alcoholic. Instead, she worked hard to raise a good son, alone.

I don't know why he picked me, but Jeff did. He decided he was going to witness to me forever. He decided he was going to tell me about God and Jesus at any given opportunity. Jeff was not shy about sharing his faith, and he made me his project. I didn't want anything to do with God because I hated him. Everywhere I went, Jeff seemed to pop up. I would run, and Jeff would follow. I would close my locker to see Jeff standing there grinning. "How you doing, brother?" he would say. I would think, *Dude. Leave me alone.* I'd cuss him out. I'd spit at him. I'd do or say anything I thought would hurt his feelings. He loved me anyway. He witnessed to me in the library, the cafeteria, even in the bathroom. I'd think, *Dude, Jesus ain't in the bathroom.* But Jeff brought Him in anyway.

I had never seen faith in action until I met Jeff. Jeff had something in his life that I didn't—happiness. Jeff seemed different than me. He came from a broken home life and was happy? I just didn't get that. My broken home meant unhappiness. Nothing was right in my world. I didn't get how a guy without a dad could be as happy and positive as Jeff was.

Jeff wanted me to go to church with him. Jeff asked me many, many times to go with him to church, but I always had an excuse.

"I'm busy."

"Sorry, can't make it."

2. *Do you ever make excuses for not doing what you should? What are they?*

_____

_____

_____

Eventually, Jeff wore me down. I ran out of excuses. He told me, "There will be girls and food." I liked chicks, and I liked chicken. "Girls and free food? I'll be there." Of course I'd go anywhere with pretty girls and free food. The night I went to church for the first time, I walked in, and I saw the pretty girls. Jeff definitely hadn't been lying about that. But I didn't see any food.

"Um, Jeff, where's the food?"

Jeff said, "Oh Ken, I forgot to tell you. We're having food after the service."

At this point, I got mad. "Dude. That's not right." I thought I was going to walk in and get fed, but he expected me to sit through a church service first?

He said, "Man, I know."

I couldn't cuss him out because we were in church, so I just thought a lot of bad words. I decided to sit in the back row, but if you want to find a back seat at a church, you gotta get there early. Four or five days early. So imagine this—my first time in church I freaked out because we keep getting closer to the front. We passed up some really good seats on our way to the front of the church. At this point I thought, *Dude, we are going to sit on the stinkin' front row!* But to my surprise, we didn't get the front row, which was already full of fanatics. Oh no. We passed the front row too. My first time to church, and I joined the youth choir! I followed Jeff right into the choir loft. Oh sure, the good-looking girls were there alright, but my first time in a church I didn't get to sit in the back; I sat on the stinkin' stage! I was in the program! So, I walked into the choir loft, and the next thing I knew, these big ol' dudes were hugging me, telling me they were glad to have me.

I was thinking, *Dude. You can go ahead and let me go, because I don't even know your mama.* But after that, the girls started hugging me too, at which point I thought, *Hallelujah!*

The night wore on, and my mind wandered, but eventually I began tuning in to what the evangelist Freddie Gage had to say. Freddie was a small man, about 5'3". He had on a three-piece suit and a pink handkerchief on his lapel. All I could think was, *Dude, what is up with this guy?* Freddie was one of those angry type preachers who, even though he preached a message of love, seemed like one of preachers who yelled everything they said. Freddie yelled, "God loves you!" He looked ticked. Then I thought, *What would he look like if he hated me?* The more Freddie preached, the madder I got. This guy ran from one side of the stage to the other. Freddie had a lot of energy, and he may have said a lot of other things, but the only thing I heard was, "You're going to Hell!"

He would run to the other side of the stage and say it again. Then the church members would say, "Amen!" I came for free food, and now I was in the choir, hungry, freaking out, and going to Hell. Freddie kept preaching, and the church kept responding with "Hallelujahs" and "Amens."

The next thing I knew, Freddie turned around and pointed to the choir loft. He pointed straight at me. "You." I couldn't duck, so I just grinned. I don't know why, but he pointed straight at me when he said, "Some of you have been convicted." At this point, I thought I would just like to kill Jeff for bringing me. I thought Jeff might have told Freddie to point at me or something. No amens or hallelujahs for that. Instead, as he pointed at me, I was the only one in the building who did this—I raised my hand in the air. I had been to jail. Convicted sounded better than the alternative. So my hand was up, and when I looked around, I realized that nobody else had their hand up. I thought, *Dude, I'm busted. They know I came for free food.*

All of a sudden, Freddie said, "Bow your heads, I'm going to give an invitation."

At this point I thought, *Hey, we're all going to a party.* So while my head was bowed for this invitation, I started peeking, thinking that a deacon or somebody

44

was going to sneak on stage and get me. "There's the convicted one right there." I'll never forget, Freddie asked this, "Are you tired of running?" As I had listened to Freddie preach, I felt a tug on my heart, the draw of God working on my heart, calling me to salvation. I thought about running and my choices. I realized that I chose to run from everything and that I had been running all my life. I started crying at this point, and I never cried at anything because my life had been such Hell on Earth. I knew it was time to make a choice. I was crying, Jeff was crying while he prayed for me.

Freddie said, "If you're tired of running, step forward." I chose to stand up and go forward. It was like the Red Sea parted, and all of the people in the choir moved so I could walk forward to the little preacher. Next thing I knew, I was standing, rather towering, over Freddie, and I'll never forget what he said. He reached up and stuck his finger in my face and said, "Son."

I thought, *Dude, you ain't my daddy.*

Freddie continued, "Do you know that you're a sinner?" God chose that night to make me His. I could choose to continue down the wide road to Hell, or I could accept the love of a living God and have, for the first time, a relationship with a Father.

That night, I realized that I was a sinner, but that I could be washed clean by accepting Jesus Christ into my heart.

3. *Do you know that you're chosen by a God who loves you? Get a Bible and read Deuteronomy 30:1 and 1 Corinthians 1:26-28. How and why has God chosen you?*

_____

_____

_____

_____

I went to church with Jeff, accepted Jesus into my heart, and I've never been the same. The decision was not about going to church, but about choosing to accept Jesus into my life. I learned that no matter my past choices, the choices my mom made, or the choices my dad made, the only choice that mattered now was Jesus. The only choice that mattered was whether or not I would accept Him. The only person whose choice mattered was me. Even though my past screamed out that I should not be the man I am today, I made a choice. I chose to accept Jesus. I chose God to be my Father. Instead of continuing down the negative road I had been on, I began a new life because I had just made the most important choice I could make. My future changed drastically.

4. Read 2 Corinthians 4. How does Jesus change your
   future?

_____

_____

_____

_____

Making the Right Choices

"Don't you realize that you become the slave of whatever you choose to obey? You can be a slave to sin, which leads to death, or you can choose to obey God, which leads to righteous living."
Romans 6:16 (NLT)

In the previous chapters, you read about how one choice can affect your family, your friends, your future, and your faith. In the rest of this book, I want to talk you to you about the most important choice you will ever make. This choice is bigger than any other choice in your life. It's bigger than choosing whom you marry, where to go to college, what job you will have. This choice affects not only your friends and family, it affects your faith and changes your future in a big way. This is the only choice that will change your life forever. Make right choices. Choose life. Choose to love the Lord your God. Choose to obey Him today. We were created more uniquely than anything else. A dog can't wake up in the morning and say, "Dude, I'm choosing to be a cat today."

A dog will always be a dog. It can't wake up one

morning and decide not to walk on a leash, not to use a tree, not to fetch and roll over because now it's a cat and would prefer to use a litter box.

You know why? Because a dog does not have the power to choose. You and I were created for Choices 101, and today, you're going to make some powerful choices. Take a minute now and reflect on the choices you made from the time you woke up to the moment you started reading this book. Do you understand that you are in school? Choices 101. Choose life or death, blessings or curses, prosperity or defeat. You were created with the power to choose.

If you choose to obey God and accept His Son, Jesus Christ, then you choose righteousness. If you continue to choose the path of sin, then you choose the path that leads to eternal death.

1. What will you choose to do today to positively affect your future?

_____

_____

_____

You read about a time in my life when I didn't get chosen. Maybe you can relate to the feelings that not being chosen brings about. You don't feel like you fit in.

You don't feel talented. I think of someone from my son's past who also didn't feel talented and who never got chosen.

In fifth grade, my son Jeremy had a classmate named Andy. Andy had the mind of a first grader. One day Jeremy came home and said, "Dad, Andy always wants to be on my team. He can't run. He can't catch a cold, let alone a football. He always wants me to choose him."

He said, "Dad, what do you think I ought to do?"

I told him, "Jeremy, I'm not really going to tell you. Instead, I want you to worry about what God wants you to do."

The next day, when I picked up Jeremy from school, I noticed he was crying. I said, "Jeremy, what happened?"

Jeremy answered, "Dad, today at recess, I chose Andy first to be on my football team. Everyone thought I had leprosy, that I was crazy or something. But you know what, Dad? I chose him. I chose Andy. The game went on. I didn't throw Andy the first pass. I didn't even look Andy's way, even though he was on my team. The game was tied."

My fifth grade son told this story to me, "Dad, I thought, there's got to be more God wants me to do than just put Andy on my team. The last play of the game, with Andy standing in the corner, I made a choice. I pretended to throw the football to my friend,

Michael, but I threw it to Andy instead. And you know what Dad? He caught it. He ran so slow, but I ran up in front of him, even blocked a couple of guys. Andy scored a touchdown. He spiked the ball, which then hit him in the head. But you know what happened?

As recess ended and we walked back to class, Andy said to me, 'Jeremy, listen. I know you don't think I'm very smart. I know you don't think I'm very athletic, and I know you don't really want to be my friend, but I want to thank you for choosing me to be on your team. Thanks.'"

Again, this came from my fifth grade son. This made me think. Every day, there are people just like Andy who are waiting to be chosen for something. I met Andy when he was in ninth grade at a movie. I asked him, "Andy, how's it going? You caught any footballs lately?"

Andy said to me, "You know that's the only time I've ever gotten chosen to be on somebody's team."

Andy had never forgotten the one time he was chosen.

Don't you ever forget that you've been chosen as well by a living God who loves you. I have proof for you today that when God chose teams, He chose you. Why? Because He loves you and He cares about you, no matter what your background is. God chose you. You may not have much money. Your parents may not have the best life. You may come from a broken home like so many other people in America.

I come from that too, but you know what? God chose me, Ken Freeman, and He chose you to be on His team. Look at this example from the Bible to see how much God loves you and chooses you with your faults, no matter what your background is.

2. Read Ephesians 1:4-14. It tells us that long before the world was created, God chose us to be on his team. What has always been God's unchanging plan? What does God want from you?

_____

_____

_____

_____

You know, I used to belong to the devil. Now I'm the King's Kid. Why? Because God chose Ken Freeman. He chose me to be on His team. He chose you to be on His team.

3. Read John 15:16. God chose you. What do you think God's plan for your life is?

_____

_____

_____

The Bible says that the Holy Spirit chooses whom He'll give His gifts to. The Bible says that Jesus said, "I choose you." The Bible says that from the foundation of this world, He chose you. Why don't you choose Him today? You see in choosing teams, somebody has to choose.

The bottom line is this: we don't need to fight to be on God's team. He has already chosen us. We don't have to worry about how athletic, talented, or smart we are. We don't have to be embarrassed about our pasts. We don't have to be ashamed of anything we've done because He already knows, and He loves us anyway. When God chose teams, He chose you.

4. Read 1 Corinthians 1: 26-28. Who did God choose for His team? Did He choose only the rich, satisfied people? No. Who did God choose? Explain what is said in this passage.

_____

_____

_____

When God said, "What can I do to get people on my team?" He chose his Son to die for them—for you—for me. Why don't you choose today to be on God's team? Why don't you choose to live for Him? You want to be chosen first? God chose you.

Choosing a Better Life

"You can choose a bitter life, or you can choose a better life."

The power of a choice. You know, we talked about it, choosing teams. God chose us to be on His team. Whose team will you choose to be on today? How will you play the game today? Which team will you be on? Which way will you go? How are you going to live?

Throughout this book, I've explained how we are all just one choice away from a different life. One choice can change everything. I even wrote about how my dad chose to walk out of my life when I was four years old. I grew up in an unstable home. After many years of traveling and speaking about how Jesus changed my life, I made the choice to find my dad. In 1998, at the age of forty-six, I met my dad for the first time since I was a kid. I flew to San Francisco with my wife and oldest son to meet my dad at his home. We hugged. We cried. We caught up on what had happened in the last forty-two years. I shared the Gospel with my dad, but he said he was too old to change.

After that first meeting, I kept in touch with my dad the best I could. We sent him cards, letters, and called occasionally. I always made it a priority to tell my dad what Christ was doing in my life. In 2004, I got a call from my dad's wife who told me that Dad had been diagnosed with liver and bone cancer. Doctors said he only had five to six months left to live.

My dad's body deteriorated, and he eventually had to take a lot of pain medications that left him sedated most of the time. As soon as we could, my wife, Debbie, and I flew to San Francisco. It was right at the beginning of my busy summer camp season.

On June 1, Debbie and I picked up some KFC for my dad and headed over to his house. As we sat at the table to eat the food, I prayed with my dad for the first time as we blessed our food.

I had the opportunity to ask my father, "Dad if you were to die today, would you go to heaven?" After we had eaten, Dad looked sick and weak. I took him back to the bedroom and asked him if I could pray with him. He agreed, and when I had finished praying, Debbie, Dad's wife Maxine, and I were all crying.

I got to share the Gospel with my Dad that day. He said he believed that Jesus loved him, died for him, and rose from the dead. His biggest problem was that he didn't want to be a deathbed convert. He hated the idea, but I explained to him that God can change a person in any way, at any time if you believe what the Bible says.

I prayed with my Dad, and he accepted Jesus. Twelve days later my dad told Maxine he had seen Jesus in the room with him and that he would like to fall asleep and never wake up. My dad did exactly that. He missed Hell by twelve days. At the age of seventy-eight, my dad who had walked out on his family, whom I had resented most of my life, gave his life to Jesus. God chose me. God chose my Dad. God chose you.

We can look through a lot of scripture for support as to the power of choice. For example, look at Samson. Samson is someone whose one choice affected his life. Samson chose women, and he chose disobedience. He came from an incredible heritage of faith. Samson could have been great. Samson chose Jezebel and that eventually cost him his life.

Another example of someone whose one choice affected his entire life is David. Think of the story of David and Goliath. David made the choice to stand against the Giant in his life. Nobody else would make that stand, but David made it. Nobody else would fight Goliath. David fought him and won. There is power in one choice. David's was a powerful choice. He became an incredible man of God who would later be the King of Israel.

1. *Read 1 Samuel 17: 1-58. Think about how David's choice to stand up to Goliath was a powerful one. Do you have courage like David to make a powerful choice today? Is there a giant (drugs, sex, alcohol, lies etc.) in your life that you can choose to walk away from? How can you be like David?*

_____

_____

_____

_____

_____

    Later in his life, David made another major choice, and his future changed. David was supposed to be in battle with the other kings, but David chose to stay at home. One day, David got out of bed and looked over to where a woman named Bathsheba was taking a bath. He told one his men, "Hey, I want to be with that woman." One choice. You see, there's power in a choice. He looked, he was lazy, and he lusted. The Bible says that Bathsheba came and laid with him. The next verse said, "Uriah, who was Bathsheba's husband, was away at war."

    Bathsheba sent David a message, telling him that

she was pregnant. They had only been together one time. You've heard adults say this—it just takes one time. Only one time. One choice.

David and Bathsheba made a choice. Uriah, Bathsheba's husband came back. David felt a little guilty, and asked him, "Hey dude, how's the battle going? Here's what you should do. Go lay with your wife. You haven't been with her in a while."

David was thinking, "They'll go to bed together; they'll have sex. Uriah can think that he got her pregnant and will never know what I had done."

Uriah, on the other hand, must have been an incredible man. His choice was character, loyalty, and integrity. Rather than go and lie with his wife, Uriah stayed all night outside David's house.

David asked him, "What are you doing?"

Uriah said, "I couldn't do it. Look at all my men in their tents." Uriah couldn't leave his men. Uriah was a leader.

Look what David did next. He got Uriah drunk, thinking Uriah would go home and go to bed with his wife. Uriah passed out instead. David was so angry, his head wasn't clear. So, he made another choice. He sent orders with Uriah to the captain of his army. "Put Uriah on the front lines." Uriah was killed in battle. Murdered.

With Uriah dead, David eventually got Bathsheba; she became one of his wives. Then God sent an angel to tell David that the baby was going to die.

David and Bathsheba made one powerful choice. Yeah, the Bible says David was a man after God's own heart. He was an incredible man, but he made a very bad powerful choice.

Today, you're making some incredible choices. It's a class we all go to. We're all making choices. Remember, you're only one choice away from a powerful life or a pitiful life.

A blessed life or a wasted life.

A bitter life or a better life.

You choose character. You choose obedience, loyalty, and integrity. We need more Uriahs in this world. We don't know a lot about Uriah, but he was loyal, he loved his wife, and he loved his leaders. Here's the bottom line. There is power in one choice.

2. You can read the entire story of David and Bathsheba in 2 Samuel 11. Here's my question. What powerful choice will you make today to better your life to be blessed, to benefit from the blessings of God? You choose it.

_____

_____

_____

_____

_____

I mentioned that I tried for fourteen years to convince my mom to make better choices. But you know what? I couldn't choose for her. If I had been able to choose for my mom, then she would have changed her life and would never have taken another drink. Instead, my mom chose to continue drinking alcohol. She chose to move on from husband to husband to boyfriend. She drowned in alcohol.

I preached my mom's funeral. She chose the wrong path and she was lost when she died. Do you know what that means? My mom is in Hell. Not because she was bad. Not because she was abusive. My mom's in Hell tonight because she chose alcohol. She did not choose Jesus.

One of my half-brothers died from Hepatitis C. He died because he too made a choice. He chose to do drugs and fell into the lifestyle that comes with that choice. He made his choice and where did that get him? Just like my mom. Dead from a slow and painful death. I found another one of my half-brothers, who also had Hepatitis C.

I have another half brother who has his life together. His choices led him down the right path. In a previous chapter, I wrote about my sister Donna and how her choices affected her life as well. I wrote about how Donna called me up one night and told me that she was going to kill herself as well as her son.

That night, I called a preacher friend of mine in

the St. Louis area and had him go to my sister's house. He prayed with my sister and her son, and that night, both my sister and nephew made the choice to accept Jesus. Donna's life did change as a result of choosing Jesus, but she couldn't quite cut her ties to the friends she had. She still lived around the negative lifestyle that was killing her.

Ultimately, and I mentioned this earlier, Donna overdosed on Vodka and pain pills. I do believe my sister is in Heaven, and I do believe I will see her again one day. Even Christians can make bad choices, and Donna chose to overdose. Remember, you're one step away from a bitter life or a better life. Donna could have chosen differently.

Think about Tiger Woods and Charlie Sheen. How would they change if they had Jesus? Would they have made the same choices that affected their friends, families, and futures so negatively?

3. How does your life change through Jesus? How are your choices affected?

_____

_____

_____

_____

Learning to Garden

"People make choices, and choices make people!"

We all have to learn to cultivate our garden of choices. Like David, Judas, Rahab the prostitute, and others, we have to consciously think of how our choices will affect us. Adam and Eve were placed in a garden and like us, they had to learn to cultivate their garden of choices.

1. Read Genesis 2:15. Where did God put the first man and woman? What were they supposed to do?

_____

_____

_____

_____

Right, God put them in a garden and told them to take care of it. They were given free reign of the garden, with only one rule to be followed. Here's the deal, Adam and Eve were placed in the Garden of Choices.

The Bible says that in the Garden of Eden, Adam and Eve lived peacefully with God. I want you to focus on the choices that Adam and Eve made. These first humans were given a golden opportunity. They got to coexist with their Creator, and they got to live a life of leisure in paradise, doing whatever they wanted. There was only one rule, and although Adam and Eve made a lot of right choices, the one wrong choice changed their lives forever. The only rule that God gave to Adam and Eve was that they could not eat fruit from the Tree of Knowledge of Good and Evil. Adam and Eve could have chosen to obey this one rule and could have continued living a perfect life in paradise.

However, this was not to be. Adam and Eve chose to disobey God and ate the fruit from the Tree of Knowledge of Good and Evil. Because of this choice, Adam and Eve could no longer live in the Garden of Eden, and they would have to work to survive. Although Adam and Eve made more right choices than wrong, this one bad choice changed their future. Often, like Adam and Eve, we gravitate toward the wrong choice and our futures are changed because of one negative choice.

2. Have you ever made one choice in your garden that changed everything in your life? What was it?

_____

_____

_____

_____

I've studied the story of Adam and Eve and have read this story hundreds of times, but I've never really thought about them being in the Garden of Choices and how we are, too.

Every day, we've been placed in a garden of choices.

Lust or love.

Lies or truth.

Rebellion. Disrespect. Obedience. Respect. Disobedience. Compromise. Conviction. In your Garden of Choices you face decisions involving all of these on a regular basis.

The devil made a choice as well. The devil made a choice to separate from God for eternity, but a third of the angels chose to follow him. You've got to be careful about who your choices affect.

3. I've lied. You've probably lied too. Can you think of a time where you told a lie and it got out of control and someone you care about got hurt? Write about that time. It can be something from way back when—like second grade or it can be something much more recent.

_____

_____

_____

_____

In Genesis 3, we read that the serpent said to Eve, "Did God really say you could eat of *any* fruit in the garden?"

Eve started talking to the snake. And man, I've got to be honest, if a snake starts talking to you and you listen to it, you deserve to get bit... but anyway, Eve was talking to the snake and replied, "It's only the fruit from the tree in the center of the garden that we aren't allowed to eat." Think about that word "center." Center represents "selfish." In other words, they had to walk through the right choices, or the right trees, to get to the wrong choice, or the wrong tree in the selfish center.

Adam and Eve are a lot like you and I. They had a lot of right choices, but they only had one wrong choice. Can I go ahead and tell you? You can make hundreds of right choices every day of your life, but it's one wrong choice that will make the difference. For Adam and Eve, it was a fruit, a look, a bite, a taste.

The old adage is "The apple doesn't fall far from the tree." Our choices affect our family, friends, future, and faith. Adam and Eve were pushed out of the garden, out of the presence of God, because of one choice. The land they tended to was now cursed and would have to be toiled over.

I want to challenge you in Choices 101 that it's always one choice. You're always one choice away from a different life. Adam and Eve took the bite, and realized they were naked. They were naked before the Lord and hid from the Lord.

The apple doesn't fall too far from the tree. In Genesis 4, Adam and Eve had two sons—Cain and Abel. Abel became a shepherd, and Cain became a farmer. At harvest time, Cain brought to the Lord a gift of his farm produce. Now I'm guessing that maybe it was a mere egg, or a cucumber, or a Brussel sprout. But the Bible says that Abel brought several choice lambs from the best of his flock, and the Lord accepted Abel and his offering, but he did not accept Cain and his offering.

4. Look in Genesis 4:6. Cain was upset, but what was God's response?

_____

_____

_____

_____

Yes, God told Cain that he would have been accepted if he responded correctly. You know what? If we would respond to God in the right way, then He will accept us, every time.

Let me tell you about Cain. He made a choice to give God just some random piece of fruit, while Abel made the choice to give God his very best lambs. Here's the deal, Cain chose anger and jealousy, and then he took his brother out into the field and killed him. Now you may have never done anything like Cain, but at some point in your life, you have sinned and done something wrong. It may not have been murder, but you have sinned. Each time you choose to do something wrong in your garden of choices, your decision has consequences.

It is amazing to look at the series of events from the original temptation to see how humans fell into sin. Look at how one choice led to corruption in the world and created a cycle of evil.

1. The Devil tempted Eve.
2. Eve and Adam tasted the fruit.
3. Adam and Eve realized they were naked.
4. Adam and Eve could no longer live in the garden.
5. Adam and Eve had two sons.
6. Cain killed Abel.

And on and on the cycle has gone. Just as the original sin entered the world, I can look at my mom's life. Because she drank at fifteen, she lived a rough life and died at fifty-two of cirrhosis of the liver. Conversely, I can look at my own life and see how Jesus changed me.

1. I was raised in a home of neglect.
2. I stole, drank, attempted suicide, hated, and contemplated murder.
3. I went to church and heard the Gospel of Jesus.
4. I asked Jesus to forgive me of my sins.
5. I started living for Him.
6. I now have a beautiful family, and I get to travel all over, sharing how Christ changed my life.

I don't know about you, but to me, it sounds like we're in a garden of choices today. Let me show you how you are in the Garden of Choices.

5. Read Romans 5:12 How did sin enter the world? Who is a sinner? Some people? Just me? Just you? All people?

_____

_____

_____

Because of one man, Adam, and his choice, we all became sinners. Whether you believe it or not, we were all born lost in this world. Adam and Eve made a choice that affected the future of all humankind, a choice that affected you and I before we were even born.

God made a choice before we were even born as well. In fact, Romans 5 says that because of one man, Jesus, we can all be forgiven.

6. You read Romans 5:12. Now, take some time to read the rest of Romans 5. Pay specific attention to verses 6-8. Who did Jesus die for? Just the righteous? No. That's not what it says. Who did He die for?

_____

_____

_____

So here's the deal, Adam, with one act of disobedience, affected the whole world. Jesus, called the second Adam, with His one act of obedience, affected the world.

You know, you get to choose to be responsible or irresponsible. Obedient or disobedient. We also talked about the power of a choice. Just one choice. It can affect every part of your life. You can get hung like Judas, head chopped off like John the Baptist. I heard a guy say one time that John had more sense in his head with it chopped off than Judas did in his head while it was still on his shoulders.

The Garden of Choices—students, youth pastors, adults, pastors—we've been placed in a garden of choices. There are a whole lot more right choices than there are wrong, and we're always one choice away from a different life. Hey, Choices 101 is a class we wake up to, and it's a class we go to bed to. It's a class we live in for the rest of our lives. Don't ever forget: "You are one choice away from a different life."

What choices will you make today? To be blessed, bummed out? Prosperous, defeated? A winner or a loser? Will you choose life or death? The choice is yours.

Uncle Sam used to say, "I want you."

Jesus says, "I want you."

Here's the deal. It's not your athletic ability. It's not your mind. It's not your popularity, your prestige, your power. It's about a choice. Choose today to be on God's team. Choose his direction.

Make powerful, positive choices. Be careful of how you cultivate your garden. What's it going to cost you? It's your choice.

Leading a Chosen Life

"Choices 101: You're one choice away from a different life."

Earlier in this book, I illustrated how it's no fun to be the last kid chosen or the kid not chosen. I have proof for you today that when God chose teams, He chose you because he loves you and He cares about you.

1. Read James 2:5. Who has God chosen to be rich in Faith?

_____

_____

    He chose you.

2. Read James 1:18. Who or what is God's choice possession? Why do you think that is?

_____

_____

_____

From the beginning, God chose you to be on His team. When you choose rebellion or deception, lust or lies, know this: you're choosing teams. Are you on God's side? The devil's side? The world's side? Every day you are choosing teams. Who are you going to play for? Who are you going to play with? How are you going to play? Are you going to let the devil win in your life? Choose God's side today. Choose the path to righteousness.

3. Pray for wisdom in making good choices. Whose side will you choose?

For my job, I travel.

A lot.

I am reminded of how we are always looking for directions on the road. I remember that once I sat with a GPS, as well as a map, trying to find Buffalo Gap, Texas. I had all the right tools, but I couldn't find out how to get where I was going. Sometimes it seems impossible to find the right direction. I don't know if you ever been there—trying to go somewhere, to find a certain direction, so that you can actually get where you're going.

More importantly than me trying to get to Buffalo

Gap, I need to tell you this, as you travel in this life, you need more than just a map and a global positioning system. Instead, you need to look at the map given to you by God. The Bible is the map of your life. It will give you directions in your marriage, your finances, your health, how to love, and how to care.

The Bible is a map, filled with directions. That day, while looking for Buffalo Gap, I sat there with a map of Texas and a GPS, and I still didn't know where I was. Sometimes, the same is true for my life, so I have to pull out my map, my Bible, to determine what direction I should choose to take.

4. Read 2 Corinthians 4:4. What does it say you should use as your map for your life? What direction will you go?

_____

_____

_____

In 2 Corinthians 4:3, the Bible says if the Good News we preach is hidden behind a veil, it is hidden only from people who are perishing. When we are looking for directions, we are looking for signs; stop signs, road signs, traffic signs, maps. Mileage, how long will it take you to get to that city? What's the speed limit?

When we use our Bible, we are looking for life directions.

5. How can you use the Bible to find direction for your life?

_____

_____

_____

Look at this example from the Bible: In Genesis 13, there were two men—Abraham and Lot—who were relatives traveling together. As they traveled, Abraham was looking for direction, not only for his own self, but also for the people around him. As time went on, Abraham and Lot began to argue (sounds like a Baptist Church or a youth group full of jealousy). The two were traveling, with all their families, tents, sheep, and cattle. An argument broke out between the two men and their families.

Then Abraham talked it over with Lot. "This arguing between our herdsmen has got to stop," he said. "After all, we are close relatives!"

Abraham made the point that no matter what, they are still family.

6. Read Genesis 13:9. What is the solution the men came up with? Have you ever had a disagreement with someone that you couldn't resolve? What did you do?

_____

_____

_____

Abraham told Lot he could choose which direction Lot and his family would go, and Abraham would go the opposite direction. Abraham gave Lot many choices. Lot could have chosen to stay and work out their differences, or he could choose land for himself.

7. Read Genesis 13:10. What did Lot choose? Did he choose to stay and work things out? Or did he choose selfishly?

_____

_____

_____

Lot chose the better-looking land for himself and his family. He didn't stay to work things out with Abraham. Instead, the two parted ways with Lot choosing to take his family one direction, leaving Abraham and his family to choose from the remaining lands.

Remember this, Adam and Eve chose disobedience

as their direction, and they were kicked out of the garden. Satan chose his direction. His direction was rebellion and disobedience. He was kicked out of heaven.

You look at Cain, who chose jealousy and murdered his brother; he too was isolated from his family. He had to make a way for himself different than God's original plan for him. Look at Samson. By choosing Jezebel, he also chose the wrong direction. When David chose Bathsheba, he also chose the wrong direction. In your life, you may have chosen to turn the wrong direction, but you can still turn around and go the right way.

8. Have you ever gone in the wrong direction? Maybe you're going the wrong way now. What did you do or what can you do now to go the right direction?

_____

_____

_____

_____

In Genesis chapter 13, we see that Lot chose the good land for himself. He looked out for himself. When your direction is selfish, jealous, disobedient, rebellious, and deceptive, you're going to head toward Sodom and Gomorrah, or Bourbon Street.

9. Is there someone in your life you need to put first today? Or are you making selfish choices?

_____

_____

_____

_____

Lot looked East and parted company. When you choose disobedience, rebellion, jealousy, deception, compromise, lust or lies, you are heading East, or out of the presence of God. All of your life, you're going to be choosing: What school do I go to? Who am I going to marry? Friendships. Jobs.

Use God's word. Use the Bible. It is your map.

Let's look at directions in a metaphorical sense. Picture this: The Bible is your roadmap. You want to get from the East to the West. Lot chose the good land, which was to the East. He and his family packed up and then ended up in Sodom and Gomorrah, which God destroyed. Lot didn't choose the right direction.

You know what I found out? Almost every hurricane comes from the east and causes death and destruction. The eastern religions mess us up in the way we think as Christians. I'm beginning to think that there's something wrong with going East.

In cowboy times, people came from the East and went West. The reason? They wanted new beginnings, fresh starts. There were fewer opportunities for them in the East. People wanted land to call their own. They wanted a place of abundance of food and land to raise their families.

The bottom line is that when you choose any direction but Jesus, you're going the wrong way. Michael W. Smith sang a song called "Go West, Young Man." If you are heading "East," then you need to take out your roadmap (Bible) and let it point you "West," or the right direction. Choose who you are going to serve today, who you're going to love today.

Choose your direction. Be careful of the GPS. Be careful of the Atlas. Pick up God's Word—it's His map for your life. It's His map of *His* life. When you choose His direction, you'll be blessed. You gotta figure it out— which direction are you going to choose? You are one choice away from a different life. Remember, people make choices, and choices make people.

10. Which direction are you going to choose?

_____

_____

_____

_____

Choices Journal

Every day, you make choices that will either bring you closer to God or closer to the world. For one week, keep track of the choices you make that draw you closer to God. Record them here, and consider how you can continue to make positive choices.

Day 1: My strong choice...

How it brought me closer to God...

Day 2: My strong choice...

How it brought me closer to God...

Day 3: My strong choice...

How it brought me closer to God...

Day 4: My strong choice...

How it brought me closer to God...

Day 5: My strong choice...

How it brought me closer to God...

Day 6: My strong choice...

How it brought me closer to God...

Day 7: My strong choice...

How it brought me closer to God...

About the Author

With the ability to connect to people of any age group, culture, or background, evangelist Ken Freeman lives with a passion to bring people to know Christ and to make a deeper, more intimate commitment to Him.

Ken has been blessed with a beautiful wife, Debbie. They have been married for more than 45 years. Ken and Debbie have two sons and ten beautiful grandchildren. He has a grandchild, Trey, who is in Heaven following a battle with cancer that took his young life. His son and daughter-in-law then adopted two babies who were born to a drug-addicted mother. As he says, "One woman's trash became our treasures."

He has a passion for his ministry and he's had an enormous amount of opportunities in the United States and internationally to do what he loves most; lead people to Christ. In his ministry, God has allowed Ken to speak in more than 7,000 churches and in more than 25,000 school assemblies.

Connect with Ken:
www.kenfreeman.com
www.Choices101.com
www.wildweek.com
Instagram: @kdaddyfree
Twitter: @kdaddyfree
www.Facebook.com/kdaddyfree